Old RENFREW

by
Alison Cumming

© Alison Cumming 1996

First published in the United Kingdom, 1996
by Richard Stenlake Publishing, Ochiltree Sawmill,
The Lade, Ochiltree, Ayrshire KA18 2NX
Tel/Fax 01290 423114

ISBN 1 872074 84 7

The view from the town hall, 1887, before the advent of new sandstone tenements.

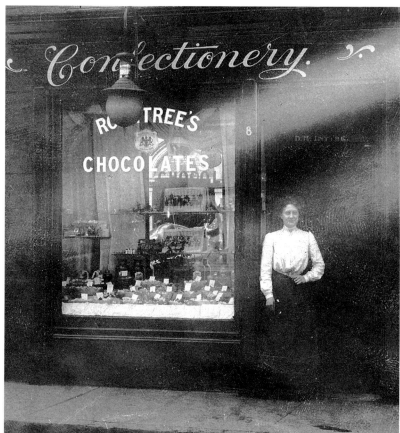

This picture (taken from a postcard) was sent by the shop owner, Miss McIntyre, although the person in the doorway is described on the reverse as 'Emily', presumably an assistant!

Left: Renfrew Town Hall was built in 1873 to replace an earlier building, and this picture shows it after it was damaged by fire and partially rebuilt. This postcard was an advertising card for the Paisley Tramways Company, and features a route map on the reverse.

The upper end of High Street, *c.*1914. This was the poorer end of the street and the buildings were built much more closely together than those at the Cross. The shops and flats on the right of this picture remained until the 1960s.

High quality sandstone buildings like these, incorporating shops on the ground floor and residential accommodation above, gradually replaced the older cottages in Renfrew. The very full tram was probably heading up High Street towards Govan.

An early photograph of Hairst Street, Renfrew's main market and shopping area. Originally called Harvest Loan, the name was corrupted to Hairst Loan before finally becoming Hairst Street.

HAIRST STREET AND CROSS, RENFREW

D 2551

The same stretch of road in the 1950s. The tram tracks have been removed and the cobbles given way to tarmac. There are also traffic islands and road signs for the new generation of car owners.

St Andrew's Cross marked the end of Hairst Street and Renfrew's commercial centre. From there roads led south to Paisley and – via Inchinnan Road – west to Greenock.

This postcard is undated, but possibly shows the official unveiling of the memorial, which took place in 1922. The clothes being worn and leaves on the trees rule out a November day, and hence an armistice service, although I can still remember attending services of this size with my father in the fifties. It's not only the colour of the stone that has changed with the years.

St. Andrew's Cross, Renfrew.

The war memorial as it is today, with the dark panel on the earlier photograph removed, and side panels with additional names in place.

CANAL STREET AND TOWN HALL, RENFREW

D 2552

Originally part of Ferry Road, Canal Street was renamed in 1786. The building in the right foreground was built by my grandfather's firm, and my grandmother spent many an hour watching the world go by from the bay window on the first floor.

Heading north from the Cross along Canal Street, the Brown Institute marked the beginning of Ferry Road. Built near to the site of Renfrew Castle, the institute had a library on the left and a tobacconists on the right of the ground floor. The two storey building beyond the institute was demolished to make way for the one opposite that my grandfather built. I have one of the chimney pots from it in my garden.

This stretch of water, which was later filled in, was known as the Pudzeoch. The meaning of the name was the subject of a great debate in the *Herald* a few years ago, although I was brought up to believe that pudzeoch meant frog.

Ferry Road, Renfrew

The same view, this time with the Pudzeoch filled and diverted, and a new railway bridge (now removed) in place.

FERRY ROAD, RENFREW.

Another picture of Ferry Road, taken from the railway bridge and showing further development. The upper reaches of the Pudzeoch have been completely filled in, while in the background the factory chimneys and the power station in Yoker are visible across the narrow channel of the Clyde.

At the tram terminus, near to the ferry, the Pudzeoch was retained as a docking area . This card is postmarked 1911.

The same stretch of water with a more modern vessel berthed this time, and the ubiquitous open topped tram car. Traditionally, employment in Renfrew was mainly provided by the shipyards on the Clyde, particularly those of Lobnitz and Simmons. The sound of the riveters went on all night, but familiarity made the sound soothing, not intrusive.

At the Ferry, Renfrew.

The first ferry at Renfrew was introduced in 1868, and this one, from a postcard dated 1905, is probably its successor. During the forties I spent many occasions picnicking on the ferry as I could travel back and forth as often as I wished for 1d and watch the Clyde go by. The Clyde Electrical Works are in the background of this picture, with steam and sailing ships on the river in the foreground.

Ferry from Yoker Side, Renfrew.

777/49

The double chain ferry was built in 1897, and took a combination of foot passengers and vehicles. It was sold in 1936 for service at Kessock between Inverness and the Black Isle, but being too wide for the locks on the Caledonian Canal was dismantled.

RENFREW **FERRY**, RIVER CLYDE

D 2553

The last Renfrew Ferry was built in 1952. No longer in service, it is now berthed up river at Kingston, and since the addition of a large greenhouse-type structure has been used as an entertainment venue.

THE CLYDE AT RENFREW FERRY, RENFREW.

93583. JV

The Clyde in its heyday, with busy shipyards and traffic on the river. The paddlers were used by commuters as well as for pleasure cruises. My uncle, who lived in Inellan and worked in the city, told of races by rival captains, but that's another story! The paddle steamer in this picture is the *Isle of Arran*.

Ferry Green, Renfrew.

Renfrew Pipe Band, a force to be reckoned with in competition, played regularly on Ferry Green.

A game of marbles in progress outside Galloway's Public House on Paisley Road.

These red sandstone tenements on Paisley Road are still standing. However, the tram service from St Andrew's Cross to Paisley, newly introduced when this turn of the century postcard was published, succumbed to motor transport long ago. Judging by the state of the walls on the left, graffiti is not a modern phenomenon.

An earlier view taken further down the road to Paisley with the tram track under construction and stopping at the green belt between Paisley and Renfrew (now non-existent). Moorpark was the most southerly district of Renfrew.

High Moorpark, Renfrew.

The same stretch of road, photographed later and now paved. This Kilbarchan-bound tram must have been held up for the photograph, and local children seem to have been drafted in as extras for the picture.

MUIRPARK AVENUE, MOORPARK, RENFREW.

New houses in leafy suburbs, 1909. The expansion of non-tenement housing outside Renfrew town centre concentrated initially in the Moorpark area.

BROADLOAN, MOORPARK, RENFREW.

Gas street lighting remained in some areas of Renfrew until the forties – yes I remember leeries, and not just from R.L. Stevenson. Wide suburban streets such as this one were a new concept in those days, hence the name Broadloan.

Bell Street runs from Inchinnan Road opposite the park, to Fulbar Street behind the town hall. The distance between the gas lamps must have meant that these streets were very dark at night.

Inchinnan Road forms the westward route out of Renfrew. The wall on the right marked the boundary of Lord Blythswood's estate, and the land is now occupied by industrial premises, large retail units, a hotel and new housing. Intriguingly, the unsigned message on the reverse of this card simply reads 'Feb 6 1918. All well.'

Looking down Fulbar Street from the station. The ornate building on the left is one of the few of that style in Scotland. Further up the street on the right is the Caledonian Railway Goods and Mineral Station. A builder's yard in this area was owned by my grandfather, whose firm built many of the sandstone buildings in Renfrew.

Glebe High School, Renfrew.

The Glebe High School was built by my grandfather's company in 1908, and the architecture has echoes of Alexander Thomson about it. In 1926 primary classes had to be moved from the school due to increases in pupil numbers. Despite the addition of various extensions and new buildings, the Glebe School was eventually demolished, much to my mother's chagrin, and a new one built in 1965.

Moorpark School, Renfrew.

Moorpark School was built at the turn of the century, and latterly housed the infant department of the Glebe school. I spent my second year there, although due to the war the first was spent, complete with gas mask, in a church hall on Paisley Road.

The Testimonial School, now demolished, was gifted by Lord Blythswood and opened in 1843. An extension (right) was built in 1866. The small town of Renfrew had four other schools, St James's, Inchinnan, Moorpark and Renfrew High (known locally as the Glebe).

Manse Street led off Canal Street. The house on the right with the thatched roof stood at the corner of High Street facing the town hall, and is visible on the right of the picture on the title page.

Queen Street connects High Street and Glebe Street, and until comparatively recently one could meet a herd of cows being brought in from fields on the outskirts of town to the dairy there (in the foreground). I visited the byre once a year with my father and a wheel-barrow – we grew wonderful potatoes!

The 'new' jail was built in 1910 and now serves as the town police station. I used to take lost dogs here as a child in the hope that they would not be claimed and I could keep them, but they were always collected or 'had escaped'. My mother knew what I was up to!

North Gates, Robertson Park, Renfrew

JV 74620

Robertson Park stands opposite the jail, and its gates are said to mark the place where soldiers were marshalled by the steward at the battle of Renfrew in 1164. Robertson, who died in 1884, was a surgeon, the first to condemn the water supply at the time of the cholera outbreak. He was a forward-thinking man, and in addition to medical interests also had shipping connections, purchasing the *Vulcan* for the transport of coal.

The Victory Baths were a gift to Renfrew from Sir Frederick and Lady Lobnitz of ship building fame, and this photograph was taken on opening day in 1921. There are two trumpeters playing on the roof of the jail to mark the occasion. In my day the baths were overseen by a 'Baths Master' who gave me swimming lessons and ruled with a (kindly) rod of iron.

The Baths, Renfrew

The baths were Spartan, even in the forties. Along each side of the very cold pool were changing cubicles with half doors and green canvas curtains. There were no showers, but three hot tubs which at a push took three shivering children each! A chittery bite (an after-swimming snack) really lived up to its name. There were no waves or flumes, but we queued up to get in every Saturday nevertheless, and the galas were always sell-out events. Hot baths were available in the basement of the building.

RENFIELD STREET, RENFREW.

North U.F. Church, Renfield Street, Renfrew

Above: The North Church in Renfield Street, to which I belonged, was the first Free Church to be built in Scotland at the time of the disruption in 1843. Its minister, Dr MacFarlan, and most of the kirk session left the Parish Church and he became the first minister of Renfrew North United Free Church. The present building was erected in 1882 after a fire destroyed the original. There was a friendly rivalry between several of Renfrew's churches, especially between their various amateur dramatic clubs which thrived in the fifties and sixties. Exchanges such as 'Are you Trinity?,' 'No – I'm Parish', were commonplace.

Left: Renfield Street and North Church *c.*1910, with new sandstone tenements in evidence. The street was named after the mansion house of that name which preceded Blythswood House.

Parish Church, Renfrew.

The view across the High School playing fields to the landmark spire of the Parish Church. The present building dates from 1862, and an old bell, discovered when the foundations were being laid, may have belonged to the first Parish Church (1726-1860). An early mention of Renfrew church appears in a papal register which names Gerard of Rome as being rector in 1247.

Monkdyke House in Alexandra Drive was built in 1897 for Col. Walter Brown. It was later gifted to the town and used as the council chambers from 1951 until subsequent local government reorganisation. It is currently used for sheltered housing.

Blythswood House, Renfrew

Blythswood House and estate were owned by Sir Archibald Campbell (later Lord Blythswood), a descendant of the Campbells of Argyll. Built in 1820, famous visitors to the house included Sir Walter Scott and King Edward and Queen Alexandra (who were Prince and Princess of Wales at the time). When Queen Victoria opened the City Chambers in Glasgow and visited the Great Exhibition in 1888 she stayed at Blythswood House, which is sadly no longer standing.

BABCOCK & WILCOX. L^{TD} MARINE WORKS, MOORPARK, RENFREW

In addition to the shipyards, Babcock and Wilcox was a major employer in Renfrew. The company, which was of American origin, produced boilers and engines for ships in Clydebank, later expanding to Renfrew. Caledonian Railway trucks, probably from the depot in Fulbar Street, (page 30), stand outside the sheds.

Babcock & Wilcox Ltd, Workers Coming Out, Renfrew.

Alternative ways of telling the time in Renfrew included listening for the Babcock's whistle, the shipyard's siren or the school bell, although I can still hear my mother asking 'What's the time on the town hall clock?' My father was a draughtsman in the drawing office of Babcock's, and I remember marvelling over the details of drawings for the boilers for Braehead Power Station.

The proud staff of Renfrew Co-op Branch No.1, at the corner of Ferguson Street and Inchinnan Road. Signs in the window advocate 'Shieldhall Tobaccos, Jams, Jellies and Marmalades'. The giant Shieldhall manufacturing and wholesaling works in Govan supplied all manner of things to branches of the Scottish Co-operative Wholesale Society.

Another branch of the Co-op at the corner of Thomson Terrace and Thomson Street in Moorpark, this time the 'Fleshing, Grocery and Provisions Departments'.

There had been a flying school at Renfrew with runways since World War One, although this Gipsy Moth would have had no need of them, being able to take off from a relatively rough surface over a short distance. The famous aviation couple, Amy Johnson and Jim Mollison, began their honeymoon from Renfrew in July 1932.

BOARDING A B.E.A. VISCOUNT, RENFREW AIRPORT, SCOTLAND   D 5168

After the Second World War, Renfrew airport expanded dramatically, and with two proper runways and an eye-catching new terminal complex was able to cater for the growing commercial market. British European Airways eventually combined with BOAC to become British Airways.

MAIN ENTRANCE, RENFREW AIRPORT, SCOTLAND   D 5163

I remember meeting my aunt when she flew from London and the terminal at Renfrew was nothing more than a hangar with a few desks in it. When this futuristic building appeared in the 1950s it got a very mixed reception from the local populace, and forty years on it still looks incredibly modern. The great arch, which appeared to support the beams of the roof, was supposed to symbolise flight.

THE RECEPTION HALL, RENFREW AIRPORT, SCOTLAND   D 5161

The upstairs restaurant overlooking the runway became a popular place for dinner or high tea, and spectators there enjoyed the new sport of people-watching. Those who actually flew were a minority group. As well as the restaurant, there was a 'cafe bar' (another modern concept) in the terminal building.

As air travel became more accessible to ordinary people, bus and train operators began to take an interest in commercial flights. The bus company SMT established an air taxi service in 1932, advertising services for both business and pleasure including 'flying visits'.